Dirty Bertie

MY BURPTASTIC BODY BOOK

For Max Bryson – who has got all the Bertie books ~ A M
For Pootle ~ D R

STRIPES PUBLISHING
An imprint of the Little Tiger Group
1 Coda Studios, 189 Munster Road,
London SW6 6AW

A paperback original
First published in Great Britain in 2017

Characters created by David Roberts
Text copyright © Alan MacDonald, 2017
Illustrations copyright © David Roberts, 2017
Inside illustrations David Roberts and Dan Chernett

ISBN: 978-1-84715-675-4

A CIP catalogue record for this book is available from
the British Library.

Printed and bound in the UK.

10 9 8 7 6 5 4 3 2 1

DAVID ROBERTS AND ALAN MACDONALD

ADDITIONAL ILLUSTRATIONS BY DAN CHERNETT

Dirty Bertie

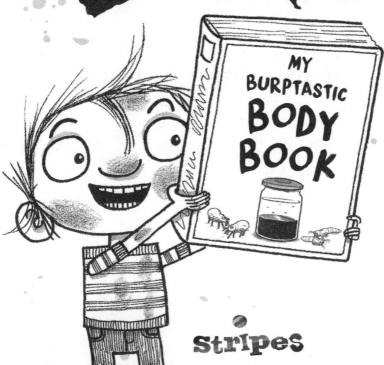

MY BURPTASTIC BODY BOOK

Stripes

CONTENTS

MY WORLD!

Meet my family and friends … and some other people you'll come across in this book.

Me, of course
- Dirty Bertie!

Mum and Dad

Suzy

Whiffer

Gran

Know-All
Nick

Darren and
Eugene

The baby

Angela
Nicely

Mr Grouch

Miss Boot

The teenager

YOUR AMAZING BODY

Ever looked in the mirror and thought, 'Wow, I'm pretty amazing!'? It's true - bodies are brilliant! You can walk, talk, see, hear, eat, breathe and sleep - all without thinking about it.

You've probably learned about the human body at school but teachers never answer the really interesting questions, such as...

Where do burps come from?

What's your belly button for?

Why are some men baldies?

Is picking your nose really bad for you?

If you'd like answers to the icky, sticky, smelly questions about the human body, you're in luck!

Read on to discover the truth about your amazing human body...

9

ALIVE AND KICKING

BERTIE

Heart beat: 90 times a minute
Brain activity: "I need a poo!"
Skin: soft as a baby's bum
Smell: old socks and wet dog
Special feature: guilty look
Body temperature: 37 °C

ZOMBIE

Heart beat: none
Brain activity: zero
Skin: rotting and discoloured
Smell: foul
Special feature: zombie stare
Body temperature: -5 °C

Actually, the truth is you could be breathing and your heart could be beating away – but that doesn't prove you're alive.

The true sign of life is that your brain is active. You may want to check on it now. Do you know who you are and what you had for breakfast? Good … then you're alive. Zombies may want to stop reading now.

BLOWING HOT AND COLD

Your body needs to maintain the right temperature to stay alive. The average body temperature is around 37°C. If your body gets much too hot or extremely cold then the results can be deadly — which is why you should never try running around the North Pole in your pants.

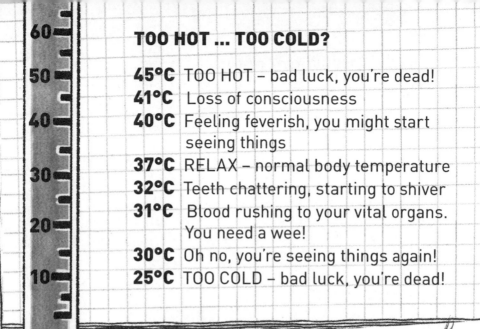

TOO HOT ... TOO COLD?

45°C TOO HOT – bad luck, you're dead!

41°C Loss of consciousness

40°C Feeling feverish, you might start seeing things

37°C RELAX – normal body temperature

32°C Teeth chattering, starting to shiver

31°C Blood rushing to your vital organs. You need a wee!

30°C Oh no, you're seeing things again!

25°C TOO COLD – bad luck, you're dead!

But what does my body actually do all day?

You'd be surprised. While you're sitting in class, doodling on your maths book, your body is busy doing all kinds of important stuff.

You might think you're not up to much, but look how busy you are…

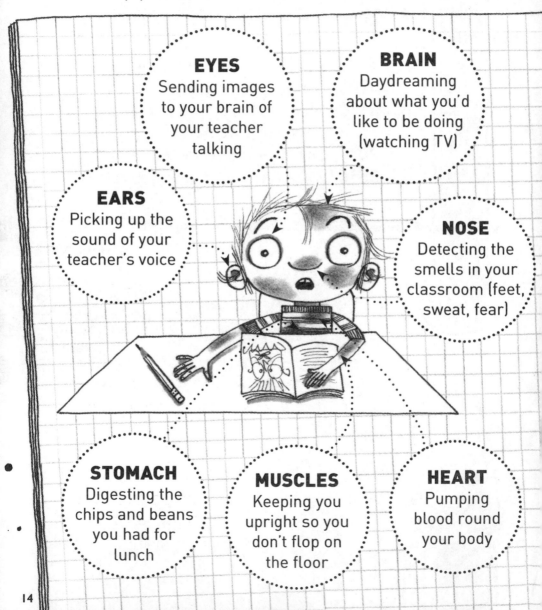

EYES
Sending images to your brain of your teacher talking

BRAIN
Daydreaming about what you'd like to be doing (watching TV)

EARS
Picking up the sound of your teacher's voice

NOSE
Detecting the smells in your classroom (feet, sweat, fear)

STOMACH
Digesting the chips and beans you had for lunch

MUSCLES
Keeping you upright so you don't flop on the floor

HEART
Pumping blood round your body

In fact, your body is always at work – even when you're watching TV or fast asleep, it's busy keeping you alive and healthy. **But what is a body made of exactly?**

> Skin and bone! And in my case a mega-huge brain! Ha ha!

There's more to it than skin and bone. Your body is made of trillions of tiny *cells* – all tinier than the tiniest dot. If you examined one under a microscope it would look like a jelly blob. Cells are the basic building blocks of the body that make up our muscle, skin, bone and everything else.

Skin and bone account for a third of your body weight. Let's have a look at what makes up the body of a typical male (a female is slightly different).

YOUR BODY IS...

45%
Muscle

2%
Other
stuff

7%
Blood

15%
Bone

16%
Skin

15%
Fat

And I thought I was 10% bogey!

Everyone has a layer of body fat under the skin to keep out the cold. Women carry less muscle than men and more fat.

But what about all the yucky, smelly, sticky stuff our bodies do?

True. There are other bodily functions that aren't so nice but are still important. Here are a few of the sounds, smells and ... er ... other things that your body makes during the day.

ICKY
Sticky earwax inside ear canal

DRIP, DRIP!
Nose making snot – about a litre a day

BURP!
Wind escaping from stomach as a burp

SLOBBER
Mouth creating sloppy saliva (spit)

PARP!
Gases making a smelly exit from guts

RUMBLE!
Digestive system processing food

It's not just you. Everyone's body does this stuff. Even teachers burp occasionally and fart more often than they'll admit. Read on, there's a whole lot more to discover about your amazing human body…

CHAPTER 2

HUNKY HAIR AND NIBBLY NAILS

Hair is weird when you think about it. It grows everywhere - even up your nose! And the hair on your head just keeps on growing! People spend ages washing, drying, cutting and styling their hair ... but I like to keep mine natural and wash it as little as possible.

Once I got Eugene to cut my hair to save a trip to the barber's and Dad went mad! He said I looked like a moulting sheep!

So what I want to know is: what's the point of hair?

HAIR FOR GOOD

By far the hairiest part of your body is your head, which has over 100,000 hairs. But there are millions more on your body, too. Hair isn't there just to make you look hairy however – it does lots of things.

- Keeps you warm

- Protects your head from harmful sunlight

- Acts as a warning system – for instance, warning you that a wasp is crawling up your arm!

Each head hair grows at a rate of about one centimetre a month – and in hot weather it grows even faster. So if you were a caveman, you might have looked like this…

Not everyone's hair looks the same – the style and colour of our hair differs from one person to another and is a big part of the way we look. Have you ever wondered what you'd look like with different hair.

And though your head hair keeps growing, it doesn't hang around forever. Every day about fifty hairs fall out.

Mr Grouch reckons I made his hair fall out by getting on his nerves!

By their thirties, almost one in four men have started to lose their hair. Their head hairs don't grow as long as they did and worse, they start to fall out sooner.

As we age, our hair often turns grey, too. This is because the hair stops producing as much *melanin,* which is the chemical that decides your hair colour. More than 90% of the world's population have dark or black hair while redheads make up less than 1%.

Gran's hair is blond ... but only because she dyes it!

Cheek!

BODY HAIR

Your body is covered in around five million tiny hairs! Short, fine hairs grow on your arms, legs and chest while eyebrows and eyelashes form a barrier to protect your eyes from dust and dirt. There are only four bits of your body where no hair grows at all.

Can you guess where?

Your bottom?

No, the answer is no hair grows on your lips, the palms of your hands, the soles of your feet or the two pimples on your chest called nipples. If you meet someone who has hair growing in all these places, then beware, they're probably a werewolf…

SUPER HAIR

Your hair is really tough. If you don't believe it, try pulling one of your hairs in two.

Owww!

Er, not while it's still growing on your head.

Hair contains a substance called *keratin* – which is also found in dinosaur claws! A single human hair is so strong it could hold 100 grams in weight, while a whole head of hair could actually support the weight of two elephants.

That's one jumbo load!

TRUE OR FALSE?

Does your hair stand on end when you're scared?

> I remember the time Miss Boot found out that I'd accidentally 'lost' my school report. I bet my hair was standing on end then!

Sweating, feeling hot, a racing heart – these are all things your body does in a "panic" situation, when you might need to run or attack. At the same time the muscles in the body pull on the roots of your hair, making them stand on end. It's the same with cats – when they feel threatened their fur stands on end to make them look bigger.

HAIR-RAISING RECORDS

People can do amazing things with their hair – not just washing and styling it, but sometimes pulling trucks with it.

In China, **Xie Quipang** grew her hair for over thirty years without cutting it. It was over 5.6 metres long – about the same length as a giraffe!

The **longest eyebrow** hair belonged to Zheng Shusen in China, who grew his a ticklish 19.1 centimetres.

The **longest moustache** in the world was 4.29 metres and belonged to Ram Singh Chauhan in India.

Antanas Kontrimus of Lithuania had a beard worth boasting about. It could hold the weight of a fully grown woman – or even pull a car!

The **hairiest legs** competition would be won hands down by American, Jason Allen. The hairs on his legs measured 22.46 centimetres!

HAIRY BEASTS

Feeling a bit itchy? Human hair can play host to some rather unwelcome guests.

I had nits once but when I found out you can pass them on, I gave mine to know-All Nick. After all, Miss Boot's always saying we should share!

Here's a guide to some of the horrible beasts that can live in your hair.

HEAD LICE
Head lice are tiny grey brown insects about the size of a sesame seed. They cling on to hair and lay their eggs – called nits – which hatch after 7-10 days. Often the first sign you've got them is a very itchy head!

YUCK-O-METER RATING: 8

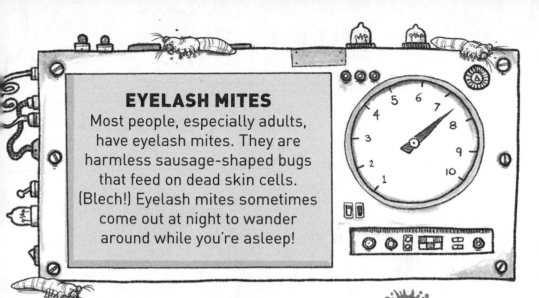

EYELASH MITES

Most people, especially adults, have eyelash mites. They are harmless sausage-shaped bugs that feed on dead skin cells. (Blech!) Eyelash mites sometimes come out at night to wander around while you're asleep!

YUCK-O-METER RATING: 7.5

FACE MITES

Tiny face mites can make their home on the hairs on your forehead or cheeks. They feed on the hair follicles (the roots of the hair). If a large number of face mites move in, the hair on your face can fall out!

YUCK-O-METER RATING: 7

HARD AS NAILS

Hair may be strong but nails are pretty tough, too. But why do we have nails?

So you can scratch your head in a spelling test!

Nails are there to protect the soft sensitive bits of our fingers and toes. They also make it a whole lot easier for us to pick things up. Try picking up a coin from the middle of a table *without* using your fingernails. Tricky, isn't it?

Fingernails grow very slowly and toenails even more so. Funnily enough, your fingernails will grow faster on your right hand if you're right handed, and faster on your left if you're left handed.

Don't worry – if you trap your fingernail in a door or whack it with a hammer it might turn black and eventually drop off, but in about six months or so a new nail should grow back.

TRUE OR FALSE?

**Mum says biting your nails is bad for you …
but is it true?**

Parents and teachers often tell you not to bite your nails but in a recent survey, over a quarter of children admitted that they sometimes do. Better still, about one in ten confessed that they also bite their toenails!

The good news is that biting your nails won't actually kill you. The not-so-good news is that it can make your nails sore.

Worse still, this revolting habit allows yucky germs from under your fingernails to hitch a ride into your mouth – and from there into your stomach.

Nail biting

Habit common in children
As well as looking terrible, biting your nails can lead to nasty germs hitching a ride to your stomach...

Symptoms:
Tummy ache, feeling queasy. *(see fig. 1)*

Treatment:
STOP nibbling your nails and wash your hands regularly.

fig. 1

Verdict: TRUE! Nail biting is bad for you.

Okay, I'll just have to bite something else!

CHAPTER 3
SUPERHERO SKIN

If I was a superhero, I'd be BURPMAN, blowing away all evil doers with my super-burps.

I'd need a superhero costume - something strong, stretchy, waterproof and super protective. Come to think of it, that pretty much describes skin.

You're right – skin is super-amazing. It never wears out, you can wear it in all weathers and it grows back when it's cut. Like the heart or the liver, skin is an *organ* – a group of cells with a job to perform in the body. The skin's job is to act as your body's protective overcoat. Your skin is actually the body's biggest organ and weighs a hefty 3-5 kilograms.

It has two layers – the outer layer, called the epidermis, and the inner layer called the dermis. The epidermis acts as your waterproof coat while the dermis underneath contains nerves, blood vessels and sweat glands.

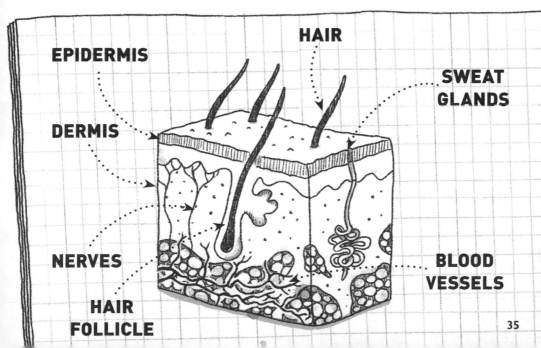

HAIR

EPIDERMIS

SWEAT GLANDS

DERMIS

NERVES

BLOOD VESSELS

HAIR FOLLICLE

When you cut yourself, the bloody red bit you can see is the dermis or inner layer.

But what if I cut myself and all the blood runs out?

It won't. Your skin has incredible super powers and as soon as it's damaged it gets to work repairing itself. But repairing cuts and grazes isn't the only thing skin can do.

Your skin is...

SUN SENSITIVE
It gets darker in sunlight

GERM PROOF
It acts as a barrier for dirt – bacteria keep out!

PROTECTIVE
Skin grows back when damaged

MOOD SENSITIVE
Pink skin turns red when you're embarrassed

WATERPROOF
Water runs off it

WASTE CONTROLLING
It sweats out nasty bacteria

CREATIVE
It produces Vitamin D from sunlight

SELF COOLING
3 million sweat glands cool you down

Don't forget belly buttons - they collect all the fluff.

That's not the main reason you have a belly button.

So what is? It looks as if someone's tied a knot in me.

Actually that's almost true. When you were growing in your mum's womb you couldn't breathe or eat by yourself. You relied on a long tube called an *umbilical cord* to carry food and oxygen from your mum.

Once born, you let out a yell so everyone got the message you could breathe by yourself. The umbilical cord was cut and what you're left with is a belly button!

Belly buttons come in two styles – an innie or an outie. Only 4% of people have the sticky-out kind.

Mine's an innie!

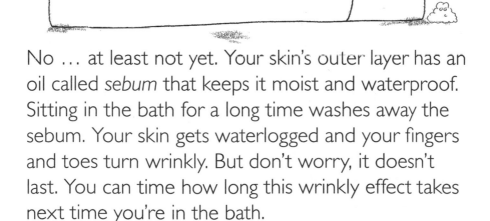

When I sit in the bath for a long time my fingers go all wrinkly. Will I end up looking like my gran?

No ... at least not yet. Your skin's outer layer has an oil called *sebum* that keeps it moist and waterproof. Sitting in the bath for a long time washes away the sebum. Your skin gets waterlogged and your fingers and toes turn wrinkly. But don't worry, it doesn't last. You can time how long this wrinkly effect takes next time you're in the bath.

TRUE OR FALSE?

Sweat is stinky.

True! You should smell Darren's sweaty socks after football.

Sweating is actually good for you. If you didn't sweat your body would overheat. To keep you cool, millions of glands release sweat through tiny holes in your skin called *pores*. In hot weather you can produce as much as 1.7 litres of sweat every hour. Sweat is 99% water. The rest is yucky stuff your body wants to get rid of.

And it's the icky stuff that makes sweat smell, right?

Wrong! Sweat itself doesn't stink. It's the *germs* that feed on stale sweat that make it whiffy – which is why Darren's socks are so pongy...

VERDICT: FALSE! Sweat's stinky reputation is unfair.

SENSITIVE SKIN

Skin is incredibly sensitive. That doesn't mean it's always sulking or bursting into tears. Skin contains millions of tiny *receptors* that respond to touch, pain, pressure, heat and cold.

For instance, if you sit on a drawing pin your *pain receptors* will definitely let you know! In the same way, if someone gives you a peck on the cheek, your *touch receptors* will immediately send a message to your brain!

Help!

Some parts of the body are more touchy than others — just think of the parts that are most ticklish. Can you guess which six body parts in the list below are the most sensitive?

1. Fingers
2. Upper lip
3. Cheek
4. Palms
5. Belly
6. Upper arm
7. Back
8. Shoulder
9. Forehead
10. Foot

Miss Boot must have sensitive nostrils - she says I get up her nose!

WAR ON GERMS

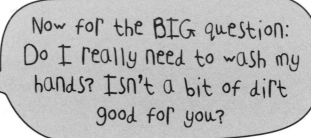

Now for the BIG question: Do I really need to wash my hands? Isn't a bit of dirt good for you?

You're not the first person to ask this question. The short answer is "Yes, it's important to have clean hands". Think of all the things you might touch during a normal day…

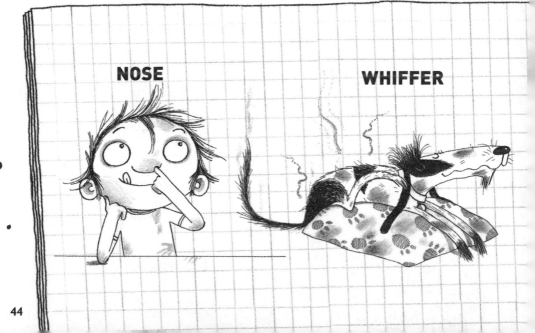

NOSE

WHIFFER

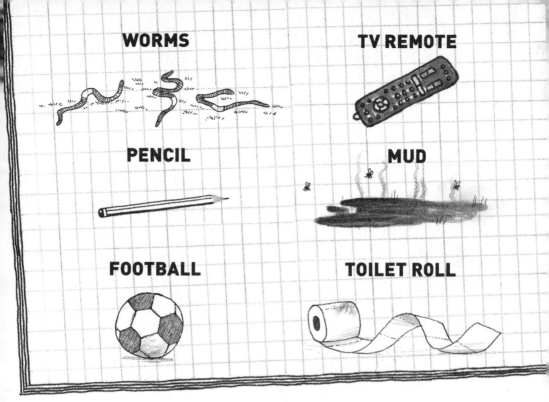

WORMS

TV REMOTE

PENCIL

MUD

FOOTBALL

TOILET ROLL

When you touch these things you come into contact with germs – and once the yucky germs are on your hands they soon end up in your mouth, especially if you bite your fingernails or pick your nose. By washing your hands often, you wash off all the germs that you've picked up. To keep germ free it's also a good idea to have a bath at least twice a week.

45

GROTTY SPOTTY

Young children have skin as soft and smooth as a baby's bottom. But trouble lies ahead when they become teenagers. One morning you wake up, look in the mirror and…

ARGHH, SPOTS!

These spots are called *acne* and around eight in ten teenagers get them.

During the teenage years, your body changes — it may grow taller, broader and hairier. You might also get acne. Acne is caused when the tiny holes in the skin (pores) become blocked by the body producing more oil than normal.

The spots can be whiteheads, blackheads or small red bumps called pimples. Sometimes they have a top full of yucky yellow pus. (EWW!) So what's a poor teenager to do when awful acne strikes?

SQUEEZE HIS SPOTS

WEAR A BAG OVER HIS HEAD

WEAR LOTS OF MAKE-UP

Of course it's always tempting to squeeze your spots but it's actually the worst thing you can do. Washing regularly and eating a healthy diet are the best ideas and luckily acne usually disappears as you get older.

THE TRUTH ABOUT SCABS

I've always got scabs on my knees or elbows. Dad says 'Don't pick your scabs!' But why not? They're itchy and scabby!

Scabs may not look very pretty but they're actually part of your skin repairing itself. When you cut yourself, special blood cells leap into action to form a clot. Eventually this blood will harden into a scab, which acts like a plaster, keeping germs out and giving the skin underneath time to heal.

A scab can feel itchy but if you pick it off then the repair work has to start all over again. Your skin won't thank you – in fact it may call you a clot.

Lots of children get chicken pox, a very contagious disease that results in your body being covered in small itchy spots … even on your face.

It's best to leave these spots alone to avoid scarring … however itchy they are!

Chickenpox

Illness common in children

Symptoms:
Small itchy red spots, fever, aches and pains, sickness, loss of appetite.
(see fig. 1)

Treatment:
Bed rest. If a child has chickenpox do NOT send them to school. Even if they beg you.

fig. 1

Oh no! Chicken pox!

CHAPTER 4
DISGUSTING DIGESTION

I love food - pizza, spaghetti, ice cream, yum! But parents have so many rules about eating - 'Don't slurp', 'Don't gobble', 'Don't eat with your mouth open', and definitely 'DON'T burp at the table'.

But burping isn't my fault - it's my tummy that does it, usually when I've just eaten my lunch!

But what happens to the food when it's inside me? I know it eventually ends up as poo but if it starts out as a jam doughnut, what happens to it? And what makes me burp? URRP! See what I mean?

We'll come to burping in a bit. First, let's take a look at that jam doughnut and what happens to it once you've gobbled it all up…

JOURNEY OF A JAM DOUGHNUT

Imagine you have X-ray vision and can see inside your body. You'd be able to watch your food travel through your whole digestive system from your mouth to your bowels and back out as poo. It's a bumpy, slippery, squelchy journey that takes over a day.

2. DOWN THE HATCH
7 second drop down the slippery oesophagus...

1. MOUTH
First stop – prepare to be chomped and covered in saliva (spit)

4. SMALL INTESTINE
Useful parts of the food like vitamins are absorbed here. The 'small' intestine is actually 6 metres long

6. BOMBS AWAY!
After about 24 hours in your body, 30% of the food you ate splooshes down into the toilet. Toodle-poo!

3. STOMACH
A 2–6 hour squelchy stopover churns the food into liquid. Stomach acids can even dissolve wood and metal!

5. LARGE INTESTINE
An overnight stop here. Water is absorbed and unwanted food is pushed out to...

BLECH! I feel a little bit sick after all that!

It's not surprising, but we'll come to the sicky stuff later. First it's time to look at your gobblebox — otherwise known as your mouth. Open wide!

GOBBLEBOX AT WORK!

SALIVA
Sticky spit is released to make the food moist and easy to swallow

TEETH
You have 20 milk teeth (and 32 adult teeth). They cut, tear, grind and crush your food

TONGUE
Your tasty tongue shapes the food into a ball and pushes it down your throat

THE TALENTED TONGUE

Tongues have so many uses they ought to enter a talent contest.

TASTING
10,000 taste buds on your tongue help you tell sweet from sour, bitter or salty.

CHEWING
Your tongue pushes food around your mouth so you can chew and swallow it.

SPEAKING
Try talking while holding your tongue. It's impossible!

CLEANING
Your tongue is your mouth's toothbrush, rooting out food stuck in your teeth.

STICKY SALIVA!

Close your eyes and think of your favourite food – imagine biting into it and the yummy taste as you start to chew…

Mmmm. A super-whopper cheese burger!

What's happening inside your mouth? It's probably filling up with slippery juices. When you see, smell or even think about food, your mouth releases *saliva* (spit) to make chewing easier. Saliva is actually 98% water mixed with a few sticky chemicals that help break down the food.

VILE VOMIT

What makes a person throw up and why does sick look and smell so ... well, sickly?

When you're sick it's like swallowing in reverse. Your stomach muscles squeeze the food back up your throat to your mouth and **BLEURGH!** you throw up. So whatever you've eaten recently will probably appear in the puddle of sick. That sickly smell is because the food is mixed in with powerful pongy stomach acids that perform the job of digestion.

Being sick is usually as a result of eating too fast or too much. You might also have eaten something that doesn't agree with you or picked up a bug. Some people also get travel sick.

Stop the car, I'm going to be... BLEURGH!

BURPTASTIC!

At last, a subject I know a lot about! I'm the champion burper in our class. But how come I get told off for burping while babies get praised when they do it?

BURRP

Burping isn't anything new. In fact in Tudor times it was considered good manners to burp after a meal to show your appreciation!

Burps happen when you swallow air while you're eating or drinking. Sometimes the gas gets trapped in your stomach and with no way out it's forced back up your throat and comes out as an ear-splitting...

BURP

Fizzy drinks make you burp because they're full of gassy bubbles. The gas builds up in your tummy and before you know it... BURP! Sometimes burps can be smelly and stink of rotten eggs. These are known as sulphur burps and can be caused by too many sugary foods or drinks.

CHAPTER 5
FUNNY BONES AND BLOOD CLOTS!

Skeletons are spooky! I saw one in a Haunted House at the funfair once and I almost jumped out of my skin. It would be brilliant if we could all strip off our skin and walk around as skeletons whenever we wanted. It would certainly give Miss Boot a fright.

Your bones are what hold you together. Without them you couldn't stand up, move or do anything. You'd just flop around like a jellyfish!

When you are born, your skeleton is made up of 300 bones. As you grow, some of your bones fuse together, leaving you with 206 when you're an adult.

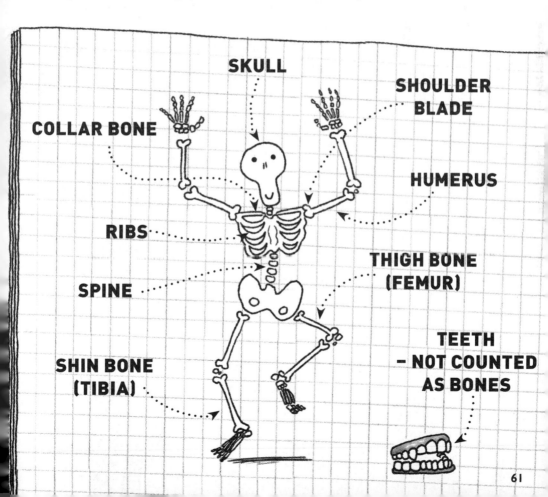

SKULL

SHOULDER BLADE

COLLAR BONE

HUMERUS

RIBS

THIGH BONE (FEMUR)

SPINE

TEETH – NOT COUNTED AS BONES

SHIN BONE (TIBIA)

BONE, SWEET BONE

Together your bones make up 15% of your body weight, and they're growing and changing all the time. They're made from stringy stuff called collagen mixed with minerals, such as calcium, which make them tough.

The outer part is compact bone which is the hardest part. Underneath is a layer of spongy bone. Like a sponge it has hundreds of tiny holes, but it's much tougher. In the middle is the bone marrow.

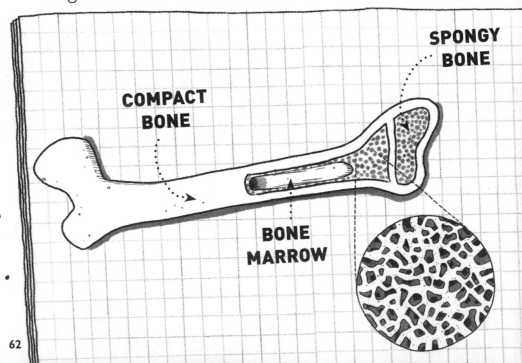

SPONGY BONE

COMPACT BONE

BONE MARROW

It's all about what's *inside* the bone. In many bones, the spongy bone protects the inner most part of the bone, the bone marrow, which is like a thick juicy jelly. Animal bones contain the same bone marrow, which is why dogs find them so tasty.

There is one bone in your body that's the toughest nut of all. Can you guess which one?

HEADCASE

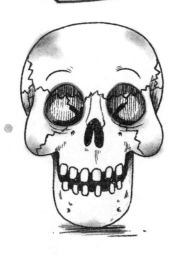

The skull looks like one big bone but actually it's twenty-two bones locked together making it incredibly strong. It's a bit like a jigsaw puzzle with jagged edges fitting together.

Your skull needs to be extra strong because it protects the most important part of you: your brain.

Scientists testing bike helmets found that it would take something weighing 235 kilograms to crush a human skull – that's about the weight of a fully grown tiger!

ARGH!

WHICH BONE?

Where's my funny bone and what's so funny about it?

The funny thing about a funny bone is it isn't a bone at all, it's actually a nerve. It runs down the inside part of your elbow and is called the *ulnar nerve*.

Oww!

If you've ever hit your elbow on just the wrong spot you'll have felt a tingling, pins and needles sensation. That's why it's called the funny bone – because of the funny feeling you get. It's caused by the ulnar nerve bumping against a long bone called the humerus, which runs up to your shoulder.

BREAKING BONES

> But what about if I break a bone?

The clever thing about bones is that they can repair themselves. Say you break your leg by falling off your skateboard or out of a tree (not recommended), you could:

a) Yell

b) Use super-glue

c) See a doctor

c) is probably best. The doctor is likely to have your leg X-rayed so they can see what kind of break it is – anything from a thin "hairline fracture" to a complete break. Next the doctor will set the bone back into place so it can grow correctly and put your leg in a plaster cast. This is only to hold the bone in place while new bone tissue grows, repairing the break. It may take a month or two and in the meantime it's probably best to take a break from skateboarding.

BUCKETS OF BLOOD

Blood must be tasty as vampires drink loads of it. But what would happen if bloodthirsty vampires drank you dry?

You'd die. You can lose a third of your blood and survive but once you lose half it's goodbye world. Blood is your supply system, bringing oxygen, food and other essentials to the body. It's pumped round the body by your heart, which sends it through your blood vessels.

Your body contains five litres of blood, so a vampire would have to be pretty thirsty to drink it all. Your blood is endlessly pumped round your body by your heart at a speedy rate…

- 5 litres a minute

- 300 litres an hour

- 7,500 litres a day (enough to fill 25 baths!)

ALL IN THE BLOOD?

But what is blood? Blood is mostly made of red and white blood cells. The red blood cells mainly do the delivery work to the rest of the body, while the white blood cells are germ busters, fighting disease. They all float in a liquid called *plasma* – which is what makes it yellow.

Yellow? But blood is red, isn't it?

Actually it's mostly yellow. If you left a jar of blood to stand for a few hours the red blood cells would sink to the bottom leaving a clear yellow liquid – plasma.

TRUE OR FALSE?

Which of these mind-boggling blood facts are true?

1) One teeny drop of blood contains 250 million red blood cells

2) Blood is three times thicker than water

3) Blood carries sugars from your food, which is why mosquitoes love it!

4) Red blood cells outnumber white blood cells by 700 to one

5) The heart pumps blood at such high pressure it could squirt it nine metres from your body!

6) All your blood vessels laid end to end would go twice round the world

7) Only the cornea in your eye doesn't get oxygen from your blood supply

8) A blood clot is a red blood cell that's thicker than normal

ANSWERS: ALL TRUE except 8. A blood clot is when sticky platelets plug a cut to stop the blood escaping.

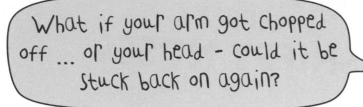

> What if your arm got chopped off ... or your head - could it be stuck back on again?

Yes and no. There have been cases where someone lost their arm and had it reattached by a surgeon. Of course you'd need to stop the bleeding – and get to hospital pretty fast, not forgetting the arm.

Losing your head is more tricky. During the French Revolution it was claimed that when the executioner of Charlotte Corday held up her severed head, it shot him a look of disgust. But this is probably just a story. The moment a head is chopped off the blood supply to the brain is cut, meaning it could only last a few seconds at most.

CHAPTER 6
SNIFFY NOSES

My nose is always getting me into trouble. My family are always moaning: 'BERTIE, STOP PICKING YOUR NOSE!'

But it's not my fault - why give me a nose if I'm not allowed to pick it? I bet even the queen does it in private.

NOSE AT WORK

Noses aren't only for sniffing when you've got a cold. Your nose does a whole host of vital jobs…

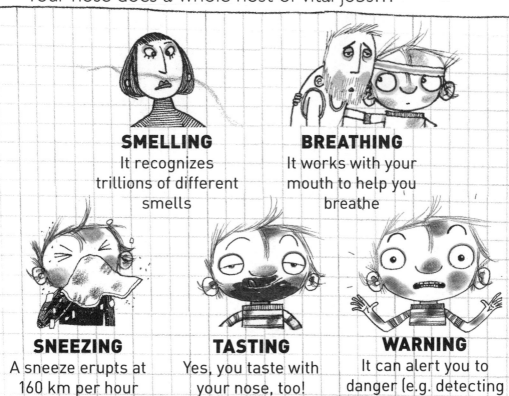

SMELLING
It recognizes trillions of different smells

BREATHING
It works with your mouth to help you breathe

SNEEZING
A sneeze erupts at 160 km per hour

TASTING
Yes, you taste with your nose, too!

WARNING
It can alert you to danger (e.g. detecting smoke from a fire)

REMEMBERING
Smells bring back memories

SNOTTING
The sticky green stuff ensures your nasal passages don't dry out

GETTING UP YOUR NOSE

It's a bit tricky to look up your own nose. It's probably easier to look up someone else's.

know-All Nick's ... you've got to be kidding!

Your nose has two nostrils. Inside are your nasal passages, separated by a thin bone wall. Behind your nose is the *nasal cavity* – which connects with the back of your throat.

Your nose is a two-way street – when you breathe in, fresh air enters your lungs and old air escapes through your nostrils. Your nose contains around 400 different types of tiny *smell receptors* – which send signals to the brain saying, "Yum – chocolate cake!" or "Yuck – boiled cabbage!" The brain has a filing system that can recognize as many as one trillion different smells.

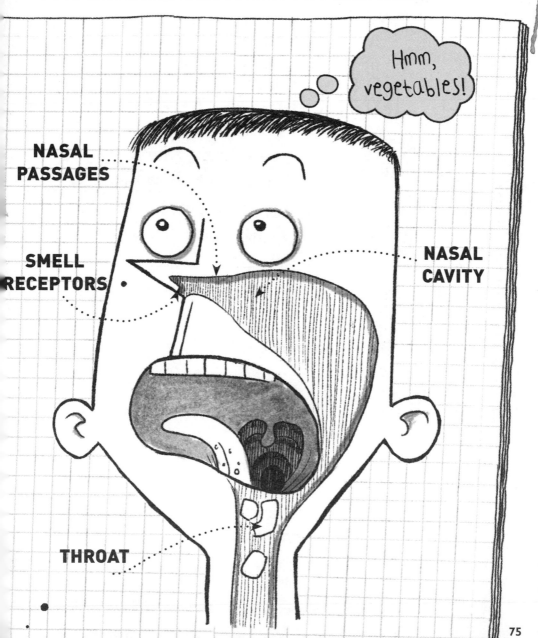

TRY THIS: NOSEY TASTE TEST

Do you need your nose to taste food? Try this smelly test to find out.

You need:

- A friend

- A blindfold

- Some strongly flavoured food, e.g. sugar, salt, honey, peanut butter, yoghurt, banana, jam, mayonnaise

- A spoon and a cup of water

1. Begin by blindfolding your victim, er ... friend. First get them to sample each food while holding their nose, so that they can't smell what they're tasting. You can let them drink some water between tastes.

2. Then repeat the test, but this time without holding their nose.

Did they score higher the second time? There's a good reason for this — although taste and smell work together, our sense of smell is actually millions of times more sensitive than our sense of taste. It also explains why, when you've got a blocked-up, snotty nose, everything tastes like cardboard.

GIRLS VS BOYS
— WHO'S THE SMELLIEST?

I know! I know! Girls are made of sugar and spice and all things nice...

While boys are made of slugs and snails and puppy-dogs' tails! So they're bound to be smellier!

Hmm... Clearly Angela hasn't been paying attention, has she? Girls and boys are made of the same stuff – pretty much. But girls' noses are more sensitive to smells...

However, she is right about the fact that boys tend to be smellier … even though girls and boys sweat roughly the same amount!

But … girls farts are said to be smellier than boys! In general, they contain more hydrogen sulphate which is what causes that terrible smell!

TRUMP

Eugh!

HOW LONG CAN YOU HOLD YOUR BREATH?

> I'm holding my breath until Darren puts his socks back on!

You can try this for yourself – you just need a stopwatch or a watch with a second hand. Take a deep breath and see how long you can hold it for.

> 10 seconds. But Darren made me laugh!

The average is around 30-40 seconds. Weirdly you can hold your breath around twice as long when you're underwater. This is because of something known as "the diving reflex" which slows your heart rate down to help you survive.

Some people can train their bodies to be able to survive underwater for longer.

AVERAGE PERSON
1-2 minutes

ALEIX SEGURA VENDRELL
(Longest underwater breath-hold)
24 minutes 03 seconds

JAPANESE PEARL DIVER
2-3 minutes

GREEN SEA TURTLE
5 hours

Sometimes though, the air has to come out…

SNEEZY PEASY

Have you ever watched someone who's about to sneeze? They open their mouth, close their eyes, hunch their shoulders and... AAATCHOO!

It's actually impossible to sneeze with your eyes open. Try it next time. But what makes us sneeze in the first place?

Usually it's something that tickles the nose – maybe dirt, dust or pollen. The body immediately goes into sneeze alert.

•Something tickles the nose. You relax your breathing muscles.

Other muscles squeeze – around the belly and in your throat.

The trapped air shoots out at 160km an hour ... spraying between 2–5,000 icky, sticky droplets of bacteria!

So next time your teacher looks like they're about to sneeze, it's probably a good idea to duck!

SNOTTY MATTERS

Now here's something I'm a world expert on - snot and bogeys! But what's the point of snot?

It's a good question. Did you know your nose produces a whole lot of snot — as much as a litre a day!

Yuck! Even I don't want to drink my own snot!

MILK

SNOT MILK!

But where do bogeys come from and why are they green?

The scientific term for snot is *mucus* and it isn't just there to look icky and sticky. Snot keeps your nose from drying up so that the tiny hairs inside can do their job. It also warms the air you breathe to body temperature and collects dirt, dust and germs, like a sort of sticky doormat. In other words, snot is not to be sniffed at.

All that slimy snot gets pushed to the back of your nose by tiny hairs called *cilia*. Along with the dirt and gunk, they form a squishy clump or bogey. The green colour is actually due to your snot's protective powers and comes from a germ-busting *enzyme*.

Of course the simple way to get rid of snot or bogeys is by blowing your nose – but *some* people let their fingers do the work.

TRUE OR FALSE?

Is nose picking bad for you?

I've asked Miss Boot this question but she always groans and changes the subject!

To start with, nose picking is probably more widespread than people like to admit. There is even a scientific term for it, *rhinotillexis*.

Dr Friedrich Bischinger of Austria thinks that picking your bogeys may be good for you – because eating them "can boost your immune system". Sadly most scientists don't agree. They point out that bogeys contain nasty germs and by picking – or worse, eating them – you just spread the germs around. In a study, nose-pickers were found to have more unhealthy bacteria (germs) in their noses than non-nose pickers.

CHAPTER 7
EARDRUMS AND EYEBALLS

Eugene's ears are teeny-weeny while Mr Grouch has huge hairy lugs. Is it true that your ears never stop growing?

Yes, it is. But the ear you can see on the outside of your head is only the beginning of the story. Most of your ear is *inside* your head. Let's take a look…

HEAR HEAR!

1
OUTER EAR
We'll come to that earwax in a moment

2
EAR CANAL
Sounds enters here

3
MIDDLE EAR
(Eardrum) Your tiny eardrum vibrates as sound waves strike...

4
...the vibrations pass through three tiny bones into the inner ear

5
INNER EAR
(Cochlea) Tiny hairs pick up sounds that are turned into nerve signals and sent to the brain to decipher...

6
The semicircular canals in the inner ear are full of liquid that helps you keep your balance

No one can see *sound waves* — but that's how sound travels. Your amazing ear turns sound waves into nerve signals the brain can then recognize as different sounds, such as music, speech or a car horn.

FEELING DIZZY?

Ears aren't only essential for hearing – without them you'd probably fall over. When you feel dizzy, for instance, it's all to do with what's going on inside your ears. The semicircular canal in your inner ear is full of liquid that sloshes around as you move. The liquid moves tiny hairs that send a message to your brain about the position of your head, helping you to keep your balance.

To understand how this works, think what happens when you step off a rollercoaster. The dizziness you feel is because the liquid goes on slopping around for a little while, even though you've stopped moving. Until it stops, the ear can't send the correct message to the brain, helping you to regain your balance.

ICKY EARWAX

And what about gooey, gunky earwax – why's it all sticky and yellow?

Earwax is clever stuff – and your ear works hard to make it. Ear wax is made by the glands in your outer ear canal – which joins your outside ear to the middle ear. But what is ear wax for?

- Protects the ear canal from drying out and feeling itchy
- Fights off infections
- Acts as a shield protecting the ear drum

Like sticky snot, gooey ear wax traps all the dirt, dust and gunk to stop it getting any further into the ear. And you shouldn't do anything to get rid of it. It will either fall out by itself or be washed away – er ... unless you don't wash.

But is it okay to eat?

Ears are delicate, so be careful about rooting around inside. And before you taste that earwax, you might like to know what it's made of…

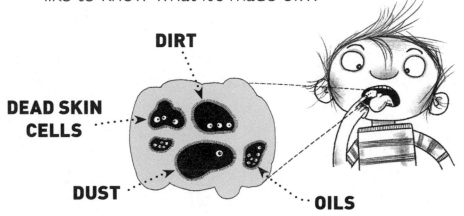

DIRT

DEAD SKIN CELLS

DUST

OILS

Feeling less hungry? In the past people thought that earwax could be pretty useful. The first *lip-balm* was probably made from earwax and in the 1830's it was also used as an ointment for curing cuts.

Even whales have earwax. A plug from a blue whale found in 2007 measured 25.4 centimetres long!

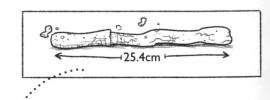

25.4cm

HOW LOUD IS THAT?

Sound can be measured in decibels (DB) from something we can hardly hear, e.g. breathing, to a sound so deafening it *hurts* your ears (anything over 120 decibels).

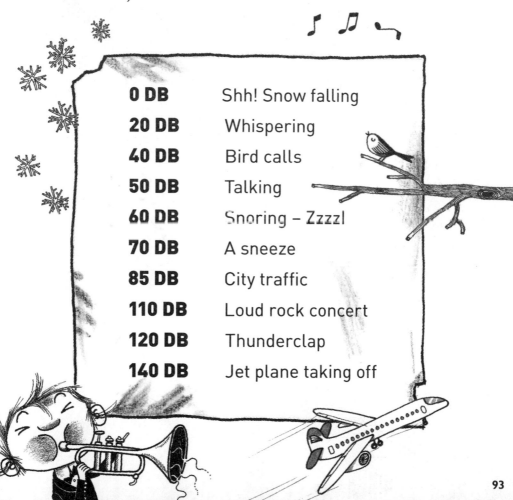

0 DB	Shh! Snow falling
20 DB	Whispering
40 DB	Bird calls
50 DB	Talking
60 DB	Snoring – Zzzz!
70 DB	A sneeze
85 DB	City traffic
110 DB	Loud rock concert
120 DB	Thunderclap
140 DB	Jet plane taking off

ALL IN THE EYES

Aliens might have only one eye or even three! Why do we have two?

Your eyes are blinking amazing – they can open, close, blink, cry and send huge amounts of information to the brain, helping you to see.

Your eye acts like a tiny camera – allowing light in and focussing on things that are near and far away. The eyeball has 130 million light-sensitive cells packed into an area smaller than a postage stamp.

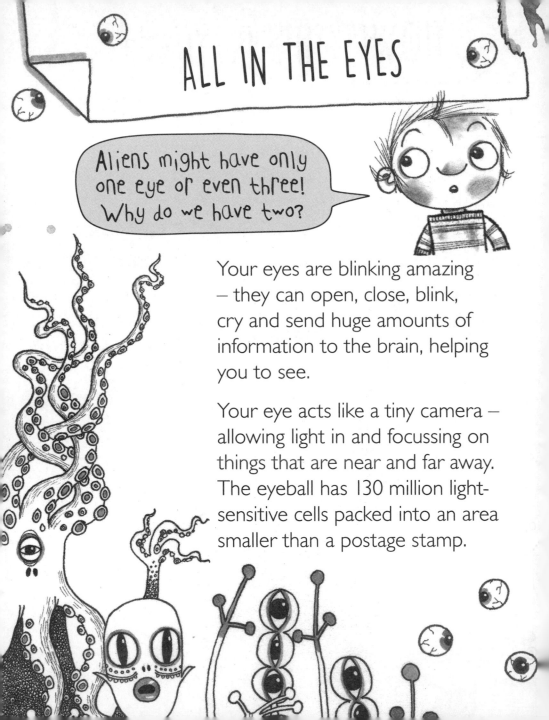

THE INCREDIBLE EYEBALL

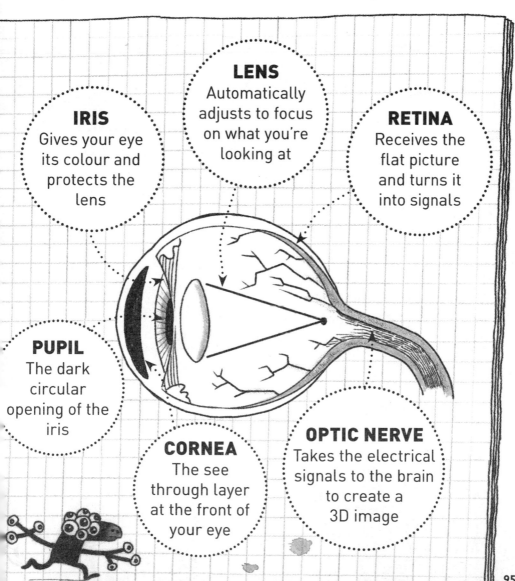

IRIS
Gives your eye its colour and protects the lens

LENS
Automatically adjusts to focus on what you're looking at

RETINA
Receives the flat picture and turns it into signals

PUPIL
The dark circular opening of the iris

CORNEA
The see through layer at the front of your eye

OPTIC NERVE
Takes the electrical signals to the brain to create a 3D image

TRY THIS: EYE TRICK

Each of your eyes gives you a slightly different view of an object – put the pictures together and you have 3D vision.

You can prove how your eyes work together with this simple experiment. Hold up one finger about twenty centimetres from your nose. Then focus on something behind it, e.g. your dog balancing a biscuit on his nose.

If you close one eye and then the other alternately, something odd will happen. Your finger seems to jump from one side to the other. This is because your brain joins the two pictures together to help you see in 3D.

TRY THIS: DISAPPEARING FACE

Stick two same-size pictures on to a piece of paper, 20 centimetres apart. Hold the paper as far away from your body as your arms will allow. Now close your right eye and focus your left eye on the picture on the right. Move the paper slowly towards you. What happens?

a) Angela turns upside down
b) Both faces vanish
c) Angela vanishes

20cm

I've always wished I could make Angela disappear!

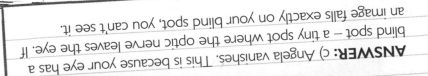

ANSWER: c) Angela vanishes. This is because your eye has a blind spot – a tiny spot where the optic nerve leaves the eye. If an image falls exactly on your blind spot, you can't see it.

CLEVER PUPILS

Miss Boot said I was a 'clever pupil' once - or was it a clever clogs?

If you look in a mirror you'll see a small black circle in your eye — that's the *pupil*. Pupils are very clever because they can grow or shrink depending on the light.

BRIGHT OR SUNNY LIGHT
The pupil gets smaller to allow in less light.

DARK PLACES
The pupil grows bigger to allow in more light.

Your eyes have two kinds of receiver inside them, called *cones* and *rods*. The cones help you see in bright sunlight. If you step into a dark room, it takes a little time for your eyes to adjust as your pupils get bigger and the rods start to work, helping you see.

CRYING OUT LOUD

Eyes do lots of other things besides helping you see. If you've ever sat through a sad film or maybe bashed your big toe, you'll have felt tears in your eyes. But why do we cry?

My mum always cries when she reads my school report!

Actually there are three kinds of tears.

BASAL TEARS – they keep the eye wet and protect it
REFLEX TEARS – they provide a "windscreen wash", getting rid of dust or dirt
EMOTIONAL TEARS – these happen when we're sad, in pain or even crying with laughter

Only humans cry emotional tears – after all, when did you last see a dog or a hamster shed a tear?

A study found that:

> **WOMEN** cry 30-64 times a year
>
> **MEN** cry 6-17 times a year

Although this was all based on reports so the men could have been lying! What is true is that women have smaller tear ducts — which means their tears are more likely to spill out.

BLINKING CRAZY

The eyes have another way of keeping moist and clean – it's called blinking. We blink so often, we're hardly aware that we're doing it.

ADULTS
15 times a minute

TEENAGERS
10 times a minute

BABIES
Twice a minute

An adult blinks around 8 million times a year!

Tear glands in the eyes are always making tears so our eyes blink them away. No one knows for sure why babies blink less often, although it could be because they sleep more. The only sure way to stop all that blinking is to go to sleep.

In fact tears and saliva (spit) are made of more or less the same things – including water, salt and proteins – which means…

Eww! There's spit in my eye!

CHAPTER 8

BAFFLING BRAINBOX

Know-All Nick thinks he's the brainiest person in the world.

But being a brainbox isn't all about schoolwork - what about telling jokes and playing tricks on your teacher? Know-All Nick is rubbish at those. I bet his brain's actually the size of a pea!

ARE SOME BRAINS BIGGER?

Some people just look brainy – like mad scientists in films or your maths teacher – but do they actually have bigger brains?

It doesn't seem likely. For instance, an elephant's brain weighs a whopping four times as much as the human brain. But when did you last see an elephant play chess or build a rocket?

What seems to matter more than size is the connections the brain makes. If you looked inside the brain you'd see different parts all busy at work. Without your baffling brainbox you could hardly do any of the things you normally do.

Let's have a peek inside Bertie's brain to see what it's doing:

Daydreaming

Don't forget to breathe!

Remember your homework!

What's that smell?

Mmm...

Is that Miss Boot on the warpath?

Wow! I didn't realize I was so busy! But what does my brain actually look like?

The largest part of your brain is the cerebrum. It's a bit like a pinkish wrinkly walnut with two halves. So you could say that you really have TWO BRAINS...

The two halves are known as the right and left hemisphere, and each half has a different job – your left side deals with speech and language while your right side thinks in pictures. You need both to make sense of the world around you.

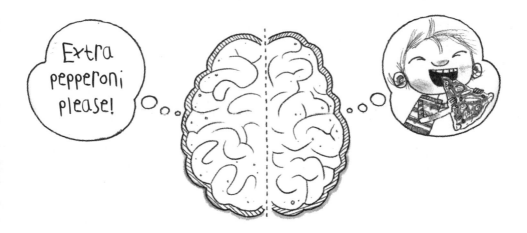

And naturally the left side of your brain controls the right side of your body while your right half controls the left side. Simple, eh?

BABY BRAINS

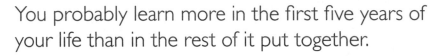

You probably learn more in the first five years of your life than in the rest of it put together.

When you're a newborn baby you can do very little at all. But over the next few years a baby absorbs huge amounts of information every day. Between the ages of one and two, a baby picks up a few words and simple sentences. But in the next three years their vocabulary expands to as many as 15,000 words.

So how does a baby learn? Scientists think that babies learn in two main ways:

COPYING

TRIAL AND ERROR

But it's not just that her brain's getting bigger, it's all about it making *connections* so she can perform increasingly brainy thinking.

So why can't I remember anything when we have a spelling test?

MEMORY MUDDLES

Memory is key to everything we do. For instance, say you set off for school tomorrow and your brain forgets how to walk…

In fact your memory isn't one bit of your brain — different memories are stored in different parts of the brain. Your brain stores information in two ways: short-term memories and long-term memories. Short-term stuff doesn't stay in your brain for longer than a few minutes. Long-term memories can last weeks, years or even your whole life. It may explain why you have trouble with spelling tests but can remember your first paddle in the sea.

SHORT-TERM MEMORY

LONG-TERM MEMORY

TEST YOUR MEMORY

How good is your short term memory?

Try memorizing these playing cards in the right order. Cover them up and see how many you can get right.

Now try memorizing this longer sequence of cards. Cover them up and try to write them down in order.

How did you get on?

I was half right – half I forgot.

The chances are you did well in the first test but couldn't remember all of the second set of cards. That's because your short-term memory can only cope with about seven things at a time. After a few minutes you probably won't remember any of the card sequence – because your short-term memory labels it as "not important". Important stuff, like your birthday, house number and the people in your class are stored in your long-term memory.

SLEEPYHEADS

Does my brain switch off when I'm asleep?

The brain is busy all day helping you think, remember and stay out of trouble. When we're asleep our brains are still very active, although our thoughts are cut off from the world around us.

We actually spend one third of our lives asleep.

- Babies sleep for up to 18 hours a day
- Children need about 11 hours sleep
- Adults can get by on 6-8 hours a night

There are actually two different sorts of sleep. They're called REM (Rapid Eye Movement) sleep and NREM (Non Rapid Eye Movement) sleep. When you first fall asleep you're in NREM sleep – this is a deep sleep that it's hard to wake from with very little brain activity. Eventually you drift into REM sleep when your brain is as active as during the day and you might have dreams…

NREM SLEEP
Little brain activity

REM SLEEP
Brain active –
eyes blink rapidly

If you don't get enough sleep, it's bad news for your body…

- You have trouble with simple tasks
- Your memory suffers
- Your body is less able to heal or fight disease
- You have trouble thinking

YAWN-YAWN

Why do we yawn?

Usually because Miss Boot is talking!

Yawning usually happens when we're tired or bored. Our mouths open wide, we take a deep breath and give a loud yawn. But *why* do we do it?

One idea is that we're taking in more oxygen and flushing out carbon dioxide. But some scientists have questioned this. All we know for sure is that yawning is catching. Try yawning in class and see how long it takes before someone else joins in.

BODY LANGUAGE

As well as speech, our brains have to read the signals from people's faces. For instance, is your teacher smiling and happy this morning or are they in a terrible mood?

Scientists think that all humans have six main emotions that show on our faces – fear, anger, sadness, surprise, happiness and disgust. Can you match the right emotions to the people below?

Suzy

Miss Boot

Know-All Nick

With Miss Boot you don't even need to ask!

Angela Nicely

Darren

Eugene

ANSWER: Miss Boot (anger), Darren (surprise), Know-All Nick (disgust), Angela Nicely (sadness), Eugene (fear), Suzy (happiness)

TRY THIS:
BRAIN GAMES

Sometimes your brain plays tricks on your body. Try some of these brain-boggling experiments for yourself!

BLIND BALANCE

Stand on one leg and try to balance. Easy, huh? But now try with your eyes closed. Hmm, not so simple? This is because your brain relies on signals from both your eyes and ears to help your body balance.

BOUNCING BRAIN

When you bounce on a trampoline, your brain soon gets the hang of what you need to do – bending your knees so you bounce higher. But jump off and your brain is still stuck in "trampoline mode". As you hit the non-springy ground your legs feel like concrete!

DIZZY SPELLS

Try spinning round and round quickly for a moment. You can stop now. Feeling a bit dizzy?

That's because the liquid inside your ears is tricking your brain into thinking that you're still moving.

CHAPTER 9

POO AND WEE

When I grow up I want to be a professor of Poo-ology! There's so many interesting questions, like why is poo brown and why is wee yellow, and where does it all go?

Miss Boot would have a fit if I asked her! But poo and wee are a big part of everyday life, so why can't we talk about it?

DUNG HILLS

It's true that all humans have to poo. So what does that add up to over a lifetime? The answer is a mighty pile of poo – but humans have got nothing on some of the prize poopers in the animal kingdom.

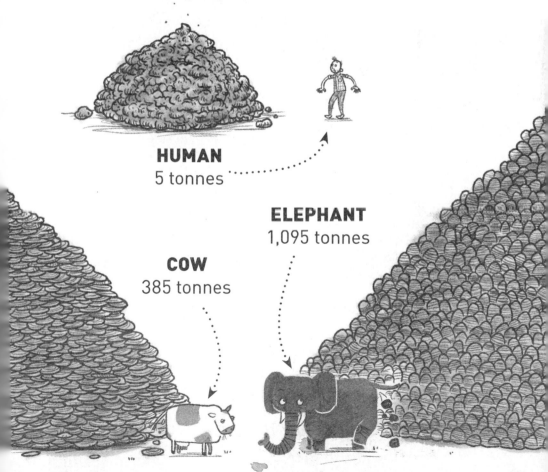

HUMAN
5 tonnes

ELEPHANT
1,095 tonnes

COW
385 tonnes

TRUE OR FALSE?

Useful poop. What is true?

You might think that poo is foul and pongy but all the same it has some surprising uses. Which of the following are true?

1. Animal poo is used in fertilizer to help plants and flowers grow

2. Cats can tell the difference between their own poo and that of other cats

3. In Bolivia, llama poo is used to clean the dirty water from mines

4. One of the world's most expensive coffee beans is collected from the poop of an animal called a palm civet

5. KAPOO! During World War 1 soldiers used bat poo to make explosives

6. Animals who eat plants (herbivores) have smellier poo than meat eaters

7. Hippos launch their poo like torpedoes to attract a mate

8. The poo of elephants can be collected and dried to make paper, while in China they produce Panda Poo Paper!

VERDICT: They are all true, except 6 — meat-eating animals produced smeller poo than plant eaters.

HOW HEALTHY IS YOUR POO?

Isn't all poo the same - brown and pongy?

Not at all. In fact doctors take a keen interest in the colour and shape of your poo because it helps them judge how healthy you are. Doctors in Bristol developed a widely used Poo Chart (yes, really) known as the Bristol Stool Chart or BSC (a stool is a medical term for poo, never ask for one in hospital!)

THE BRISTOL STOOL CHART

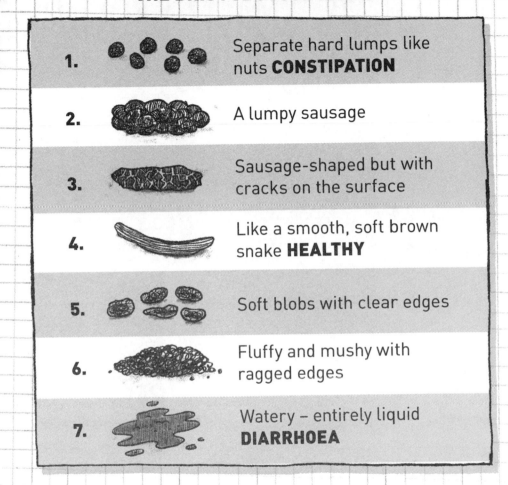

1. Separate hard lumps like nuts **CONSTIPATION**

2. A lumpy sausage

3. Sausage-shaped but with cracks on the surface

4. Like a smooth, soft brown snake **HEALTHY**

5. Soft blobs with clear edges

6. Fluffy and mushy with ragged edges

7. Watery – entirely liquid **DIARRHOEA**

So how did your poo do? Healthy poos are somewhere around 4-5 on the scale, while if your poo fits the description of 1 or 7 you may need to see a doctor.

WHAT'S SMALL, BROWN AND PONGY?

So poo can be hard or squishy but you haven't explained why it's brown?

Actually it *isn't* always brown. When you're a tiny baby your poo may be green, and eating tons of vegetables may get the same result.

Remember the journey of a jam doughnut? By the time your food reaches the large intestine all the useful parts of it have been taken out. What's left is the waste.

Poo gets its colour and pongy smell while it's in the large intestine. It's made of the waste your body can't digest, which trillions of bacteria feed on, and that's what turns it brown. Three quarters of the poo is made of water. The rest is mainly dead bacteria, which is what gives it it's pongy whiff. As we've seen though, not all poo is healthy, which can lead to some poopy problems.

I thought that would get your attention...

DIRE TUMMY TROUBLE

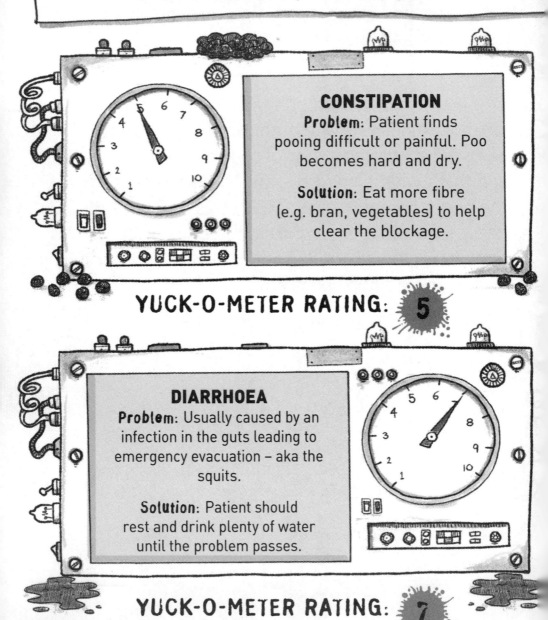

CONSTIPATION

Problem: Patient finds pooing difficult or painful. Poo becomes hard and dry.

Solution: Eat more fibre (e.g. bran, vegetables) to help clear the blockage.

YUCK-O-METER RATING: 5

DIARRHOEA

Problem: Usually caused by an infection in the guts leading to emergency evacuation – aka the squits.

Solution: Patient should rest and drink plenty of water until the problem passes.

YUCK-O-METER RATING: 7

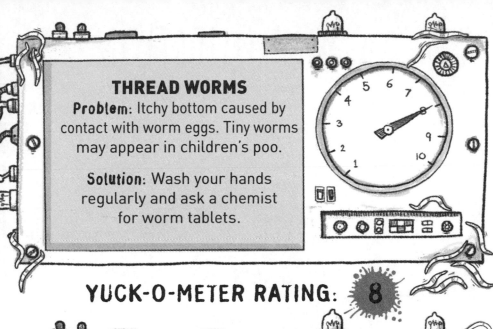

THREAD WORMS

Problem: Itchy bottom caused by contact with worm eggs. Tiny worms may appear in children's poo.

Solution: Wash your hands regularly and ask a chemist for worm tablets.

YUCK-O-METER RATING: 8

TAPEWORMS

Problem: A parasite caught from eating infected food. A tapeworm lives in the intestines feeding off the body's food and can grow up to 10 metres long.

Solution: Most tapeworms can be treated with medicine.

YUCK-O-METER RATING: 9

Okay, I'm feeling sick now! Can we talk about wee?

A WEE QUESTION

The scientific word for wee is urine. But what's in it and why does it come out yellow? If you tested a sample of your wee you would find:

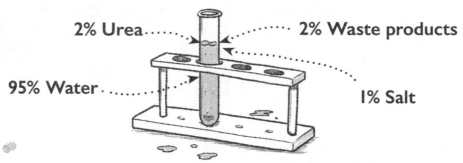

2% Urea

2% Waste products

95% Water

1% Salt

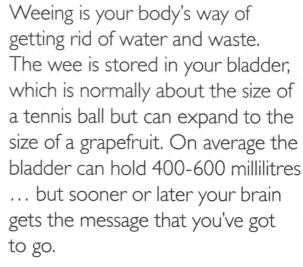

Weeing is your body's way of getting rid of water and waste. The wee is stored in your bladder, which is normally about the size of a tennis ball but can expand to the size of a grapefruit. On average the bladder can hold 400-600 millilitres … but sooner or later your brain gets the message that you've got to go.

'NEED FOR WEE'

I once got stuck on a coach when I desperately needed a wee! Here's my top tips for what not to do if you're dying to go...

SINGING – doesn't help
JIGGLING AND DANCING – no help
THINKING OF RAIN OR A RUNNING TAP – bad idea
DRINKING WATER – terrible idea
LAUGHING – it hurts!
TELLING A TEACHER – hopeless, especially if it's Miss Boot

Of course not all waste exits the body as poo or wee, there are other ways…

FOUL FARTING

Breaking wind, farts or bottom burps are something that children often find hilarious ... while teachers act as if you did it on purpose.

> Doesn't everyone fart, even teachers?

It's a fact – everyone farts on a daily basis – around 14 times on average. Parents and teachers will deny this is true but that's just because they've learned to fart quietly or silently (which is often worse). So who do you think farts most often, men or women?

Most people would point the finger at men. But actually a study found that women farted three times more often (but they're better at disguising it).

Like a burp, a fart is trapped gas escaping from your body. Just 1% of the gas (sulphur) accounts for the pongy smell – the other 99% doesn't smell at all.

Of course, you can always blame it on the dog...

If you want to turn yourself into a walking stinkbomb at school, here are the foods you should eat:

TOP TEN FARTIEST FOOD AND DRINK

BEANS – as anyone knows, most kinds of beans have a sure-fire effect

BRUSSELS SPROUTS – another farty favourite, especially at Christmas time

FIZZY DRINKS – those gassy bubbles can only mean one thing...

MEAT – takes longer for your stomach to process, allowing gas to build

FRUITS – good for you but smelly for others!

EGGS – you've heard of eggy farts?

BROCCOLI – see sprouts ... can be lethal

CURRY – spicy = smelly

CABBAGE – enough said...

SWEETS – hard-boiled sweets can cause you to swallow air – with one result!

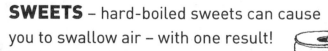

THE FAMOUS FARTY FRENCHMAN

You'll be pleased to know that farting can lead to fame and fortune. During the 19th century a Frenchman became a huge success through his unusual skill. Audiences flocked to see Joseph Pujol, nicknamed Le Pétomane, which roughly translates as "fartomaniac". His performances took farting to a level that had audiences rocking with laughter.

I can assure you that my performance will have no odour whatsoever!

When La Pétomane died in 1945, his son Louis said: "In the course of his long life, he had given of his best."

CHAPTER 10

GROWING BODIES

But I once kept an eye on myself for about an hour and I never grew one bit! Of course my hair seems to grow a lot and so do my toenails but does that mean the rest of my body is growing all the time?

If it is, when does it stop? If Gran is still growing she ought to be giant by now but if you ask me most old people look like they're shrinking!

It's an amazing thought that right now, as you read this book, your body is growing. The truth is that we keep growing for the first twenty or so years of our life. After that you stop – you've become what's called a "grown-up" and there's nothing you can do to change how short or tall you are.

THE LONG AND THE SHORT

As you grow your bones get longer, especially the ones in your legs, which grow the most. But how come some people in your class remain small while others seem to grow like weeds?

The short answer is that it's down to *hormones*. Hormones are chemicals that are released in your body and carry instructions to your cells. How fast you grow is controlled by a hormone produced in your brain and will also depend on your diet and health. For instance if you're living entirely on a diet of worms, you may not grow very big (or you may turn into a sparrow).

Although you're always growing, you don't grow at the same speed all the time. You get off to a fast start as a baby, then slow down as a child before putting on a growth spurt in your teenage years. That's why teenagers sometimes look as if they're still growing into their bodies.

A baby is one twentieth of the weight they'll be fully grown.

At two a child reaches roughly half their adult height. They learn to crawl, walk – and fall over.

Children grow at around 5–7 cms a year. They learn speech, reading and writing (sort of).

Major body changes take place as growth speeds up. Boys grow taller, more muscled and often spottier.

A fully grown body reaches its peak in its twenties and thirties. After that it's mostly downhill...

Bones get weaker, joints creak and your body actually begins to shrink in old age.

BABY TALK

Let's start at the beginning. As a baby you grow most in your first year. In fact during that time your brain more than doubles in size.

Have you ever noticed what gigantic heads babies have? They're huge!

HEAD
one quarter of body length

Before they are born, babies develop a skeleton. It's not made of bone yet but squishier stuff called *cartilage* – the soft tissue that protects your joints. That's why babies are much less likely to break a bone than adults or children. As a baby grows, the soft cartilage gradually turns into bone.

At first, babies don't do a lot – they can wee, poo, sick, sleep, dribble, drink and poo again. In fact at birth a baby can't even see the world properly. Because the brain hasn't fully developed, a baby sees double and upside down. It must be pretty scary…

But luckily babies learn pretty quickly.

BABY'S FIRST YEAR

FIRST CRY

FIRST DRINK

FIRST SICK

FIRST SMILE

FIRST THUMB SUCKING (OR TOE)

FIRST CRAWL

FIRST SOLID MEAL

FIRST STEP

POO!

FIRST WORD

In other words in your first year as a baby you probably learn more than in all your schooldays put together. Babies learn to recognize faces and voices, to copy actions and noises. Eventually they even learn how to control when they poo or wee – which is just as well for everybody else!

But let's skip on seventy or eighty years in the human body's life. What happens to the body when you reach old age?

CREAKY OLD AGE

Many old people – your teacher, for instance – will tell you that inside they still feel about eighteen. Unfortunately for them their bodies don't look that way!

As the body moves into creaky old age things start to pack up and go wrong, like an old car that's rusting and falling apart.

Remember that we said your body is made up of millions of tiny cells? Well, these are always dying off and new cells replace them. The problem is there's a limit to this, and eventually our cells reach their sell-by date. Skin becomes thinner and less elastic and that's just the beginning.

Let's look at my teacher, Miss Boot - she's really old...

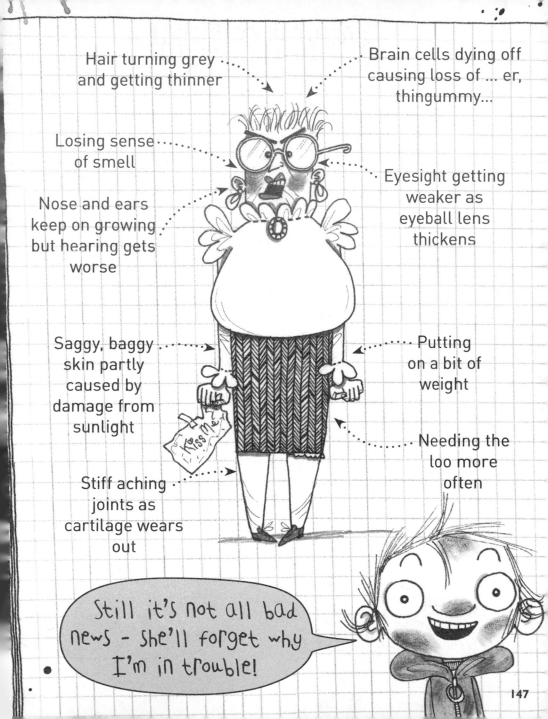

INCREDIBLE OLDIES

Awful ageing brings a whole new set of problems for the poor old human body. As if losing your hearing and sense of smell isn't enough – the body isn't as effective at fighting off illness or diseases.

But it doesn't have to be all downhill. The good news is that with exercise and a healthy diet you don't necessarily have to shuffle around in your slippers in your later years.

In fact some oldies have achieved pretty amazing things.

WE ARE THE WRINKLY CHAMPIONS

The oldest woman to complete a marathon was Harriette Thompson, who was 92 at the time. Waving the flag for men, Fauja Singh is the first 100-year-old to ever run a marathon.

South African Mohr Keet became the world's oldest bungee jumper when he jumped 216 metres at the age of 96. His other hobbies included parachuting and white-water rafting.

At 87, retired Lieutenant Colonel James C Warren became the world's oldest person to gain his pilot's licence.

Country music singer Smokey Dawson, Australia's singing cowboy, released his first album at the age of 92.

Climbing Mount Everest is a tough challenge but Yuichiro Miura conquered it at the age of 70. He went back again at 75 and 80!

Dorothy Darrenhill Hirsch visited the North Pole when she was 89, braving temperatures of minus 43°C.

Astronaut John Glenn went back into space at the age of 77 and orbited the Earth in the space shuttle Discovery. It's never too late.

Kimani Maruge started school in Kenya when he was 84. A year later he became Head Boy. (Well, he was mature for his age.)

Yikes! Imagine still having to do your homework when you're old!

BODYWORK

It pays to take care of your body — after all, it's the only one you've got. All your life it works round the clock to keep you alive and healthy, fighting off yucky germs and repairing any cuts or wounds.

Human bodies are amazing — they start off as helpless little babies and can grow into 100-year-old marathon runners. Humans have learned to dive down to the bottom of the ocean and travel into space. Who knows what the human body of the future might look like?

Well, duh! I do!

WONDERBOY

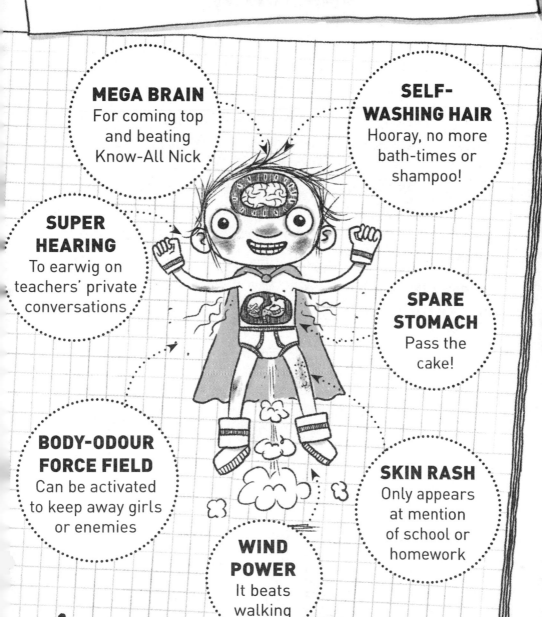

MEGA BRAIN
For coming top and beating Know-All Nick

SELF-WASHING HAIR
Hooray, no more bath-times or shampoo!

SUPER HEARING
To earwig on teachers' private conversations

SPARE STOMACH
Pass the cake!

BODY-ODOUR FORCE FIELD
Can be activated to keep away girls or enemies

SKIN RASH
Only appears at mention of school or homework

WIND POWER
It beats walking

GLOSSARY

ACNE – a skin condition that affects teenagers and causes spots, mostly on the face

BACTERIA – tiny organisms that live inside our bodies and all around us; most aren't dangerous but some can make us ill

BLADDER – the sac that holds your wee, which can change from the size of a tennis ball to the size of a grapefruit

BOWELS – the long tube (including your intestines) that carries solid waste from your stomach out of your body

CARTILAGE – the soft tissue that protects your joints

CELLS – the building blocks of the body that make up your skin, bone, muscle and everything else

CEREBRUM – the largest part of your brain, which looks like two halves of a wrinkly walnut

CILIA – tiny hairs inside your nose that push bogeys, dust and dirt to the back of your nose

COCHLEA – the spiral cavity in your inner ear that changes sounds into nerve messages and sends them to your brain

COLLAGEN – the stringy protein that gives strength to your bones and helps hold them together

CORNEA – the see-through layer at the front of your eye

DERMIS – the inner layer of your skin, containing blood vessels, sweat glands and nerves

EAR CANAL – the tube connecting your outer ear to your middle ear

EAR DRUM – the membrane of the middle ear, which vibrates in response to sound waves

ENZYME – a special type of protein that helps to speed up a chemical reaction in your body

EPIDERMIS – the outer layer of your skin, which acts as a waterproof coat

HORMONES – chemicals released into your body that carry instructions to your cells

IRIS – the coloured part of your eye

KERATIN – a special protein that occurs in your hair and nails, which makes them strong

LARGE INTESTINE – the lower part of the bowels in which water is removed from digested food

LENS – the part of the eye that focuses light rays on the retina

MELANIN – a dark brown pigment that occurs in hair and skin

NREM (Non Rapid Eye Movement) SLEEP – a deep sleep in which brain activity is low

OESOPHAGUS – the passage that takes food from your mouth to your stomach

OPTIC NERVE – the nerve in your eye that transmits impulses to your brain from your retina

PLASMA – the colourless fluid part of your blood

PUPIL – the dark circular opening of the iris that controls how much light gets into the eye

REM (Rapid Eye Movement) SLEEP – sleep where your brain is very active and you're prone to dream

RETINA – the layer at the back of the eyeball that sends messages about light to your optic nerve

SALIVA (SPIT) – the liquid produced in your mouth to aid food digestion

SEMICIRCULAR CANALS – located in the inner ear, these are filled with liquid that help you keep your balance

SMALL INTESTINE – the upper part of the bowels where useful parts of food are digested

SOUND WAVES – the form sound takes when it travels through air and water, etc.

ULNAR NERVE – the nerve on the inside of your elbow also known as your funny bone

UMBILICAL CORD – the long tube that carries food and oxygen from a mother to her unborn baby

Alan MacDonald is the author of over sixty books for children. He was born in Watford and now lives a stone's throw from the River Trent in Nottingham, where he is married with three children. When he was growing up his ambition was to become a professional footballer but then he won a pen in a handwriting competition and his fate was sealed.

He writes his stories in notebooks with lots of crossings out. He is best known for his humorous fiction and, as well as *Dirty Bertie*, he is the author of many other series including *Angela Nicely, Superhero School, History of Warts* and *Troll Trouble.*

David Roberts is one of the UK's foremost children's illustrators. His first doodles were for *Frankie Stein's Robot* by Roy Apps and his pen hasn't stopped working since! He has gone on to doodle for writers including Julia Donaldson, Sally Gardner and most recently, Julian Clary in *The Bolds*. David has been shortlisted for the CILIP Kate Greenaway Medal three times and in 2006 he won the Nestlé Children's Book Prize Gold Award for *Mouse Noses on Toast*.

There are loads of Dirty Bertie books for you to collect. Each one has wickedly funny stories by best-selling author Alan MacDonald and wonderfully witty illustrations by David Roberts.

COLLECT THEM ALL!

Dirty Bertie — WORMS!

Dirty Bertie — FLEAS!

Dirty Bertie — PANTS!

Dirty Bertie — BURP!

Dirty Bertie — YUCK!

Dirty Bertie — CRACKERS!

Dirty Bertie — BOGEYS!

Dirty Bertie — MUD!

Dirty Bertie — GERMS!

Dirty Bertie — LOO!

Dirty Bertie — FETCH!

Dirty Bertie — FANGS!

Dirty Bertie — KISS!

Dirty Bertie — OUCH!

Dirty Bertie — SNOW!

Dirty Bertie — PONG!

Dirty Bertie — PIRATE!

Dirty Bertie — SCREAM!

Dirty Bertie — TOOTHY!

Dirty Bertie — DINOSAUR!

COLLECT THEM ALL!

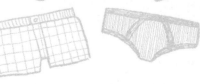

ACKNOWLEDGEMENTS

Along with countless websites, I'd like to acknowledge the following books which provided helpful source material:

Understanding your Body – Rebecca Treays (Usborne)
The Awesome Body Book – Adam Frost (Bloomsbury)
The Horrible Science of You – Nick Arnold and Tony De Saulles (Scholastic)
Wow! Human Body – Richard Walker (Dorling Kindersley)
Bodies: The Whole Blood-Pumping Story – Glenn Murphy (Macmillan)
That's So Gross!: Human Body – Mitchell Symons (Red Fox)

Pardon me!